taste.
30 MINUTE MEALS

Over 100 mouth-watering recipes

igloo

igloo

Published in 2011
by Igloo Books Ltd
Cottage Farm
Sywell
NN6 0BJ

www.igloo-books.com
Copyright © 2011 Igloo Books Ltd

B044 0811
2 4 6 8 10 9 7 5 3 1
ISBN: 978-0-85734-758-9

Food photography and recipe development: Stockfood, The Food Image Agency
Front and back cover images © Stockfood, The Food Image Agency

Printed and manufactured in China.

contents.

introduction.

Do you love good food, but just don't have the time to follow long, complicated recipes? Then this is the book for you! All the recipes that follow can be prepared, cooked and ready to eat in 30 minutes or less; and what's more, they're delicious! From fresh ideas to liven up your breakfast, to healthy lunches and dinner party ideas, there are over 100 recipes to suit any occasion.

Breakfast

To get your morning off to a healthy start, why not try one of the delicious smoothie recipes? They have all the nutrients you need to boost your energy, they taste great and count towards your five-a-day. If you're looking for something more indulgent, there are lots of delicious recipes like French toast, muffins, baguettes and pancakes, all ready in 30 minutes.

Brunch

For a quick and delicious weekend brunch, why not enjoy an English muffin, or cook up a frittata in just a matter of minutes. There are fresh ideas from around the world, such as Mexican quesadillas, a French croque madame or Italian bruschetta.

Lunch

There are a whole host of lunchtime ideas that you can cook up in minutes, whether unexpected guests have just arrived, or you're home on a lunch hour, there are tasty lunch suggestions for a picnic, such as the courgette and goat's cheese salad, or soups, pastas, sandwiches and many more light, quick and delicious meals made in minutes.

Dinner

For something a bit more substantial at dinnertime, we've got some quick and easy recipes, whether you've come in from a hard day's work, you've got plans for the rest of the evening, or you simply don't want to be slaving away in the kitchen. Why not try the aromatic Thai red curry, or the hearty sausage and vegetable casserole?

Desserts

No matter how much of a rush you're in, you can always find time for dessert! We've dedicated a whole chapter to sweet treats that can be whipped up quicker than you even thought possible, there are classic desserts like banana fritters, tiramisu and rice pudding, as well as healthy alternatives, such as fruit salads and strawberry meringues.

Here are a few hints and tips to help you save time:

Make sure you are well-stocked with essential ingredients, such as eggs, flour and milk. When you're looking for something quick and easy to make, staple ingredients like these will give you many more options.

Dried goods keep well, so you can afford to have a well-stocked herb and spice rack. The following ingredients offer a great start: mustard powder; any dried herbs and spice mixes; dried fruit; nuts; rice; pasta; noodles; flour, other grains, such as quinoa and couscous; bicarbonate of soda, cornflour and stock cubes.

Often you can freeze items, or buy frozen ingredients that will be ready at a moment's notice. Keep your freezer full of frozen fruits and vegetables, as well as handy stocks and soups.

Make sure your workspace is tidy and you feel comfortable in the kitchen. Keep equipment you use often close at hand and try to tidy as you go.

Make sure you've got the right equipment for the job, as this will save you a lot of time and stress. Keep your knives sharp, they will chop more efficiently and it is safer and easier.

Plan ahead, this will save time and worries later on – you can even cook food ahead of time and heat it up when you need it.

Try making double and freezing half of the portion, such as curries and casseroles, it doesn't take much longer and you'll have a tasty meal ready for when you haven't got any time at all to cook.

If your butcher of fishmonger offers services such as skinning, trimming and boning – take advantage of these, make use of their skills to save yourself time and stress in the kitchen.

All of the recipes that follow, look good, taste fabulous and can all be prepared in less than 30 minutes, so what are you waiting for?

breakfast.

Egg and bacon muffins

serves: 4

Ingredients:
4 eggs
2 English muffins, split in half and toasted
1 tbsp butter
12 slices streaky bacon

Method:

Heat the grill and cook the bacon on both sides until crisp.

Place the eggs in a pan of boiling, salted water. Boil for 4 minutes and remove them from the pan.

Spread the toasted muffins with the butter and place 3 slices of bacon on each muffin half.

Peel off the egg shells and place the eggs on top of the bacon and serve immediately.

French toast with fresh fruit salad

serves: 4

Ingredients:
1 small pineapple, peeled,
cored and sliced
1 pink grapefruit, peeled and sliced
1 small honeydew melon, peeled,
deseeded and chopped
200 g | 7 oz strawberries,
hulled and sliced
3 eggs
125 ml | 4 ½ fl. oz | ½ cup milk
1 tbsp sugar
30 g | 1 oz butter
4 slices bread
sugar, to serve

Method:
Mix all the fruit together and set it aside. Beat the eggs with the milk and the sugar.

Heat the butter in a frying pan until bubbling. Dip the bread into the egg mixture and fry in batches for 2-3 minutes on each side until golden brown.

Slice the bread in half diagonally and place on serving plates. Spoon over the fruit and sprinkle a little sugar to serve.

Blueberry muffins

makes: 12

Ingredients:
110 g | 4 oz | ½ cup butter, softened
75 g | 2 ½ oz | ⅓ cup sugar
3 eggs
110 g | 4 oz | 1 cup plain
(all-purpose) flour
2 tsp baking powder
100 g | 3 ½ oz | 1 cup blueberries
75 g | 2 ½ oz | ½ cup ground almonds

Method:

Heat the oven to 200°C (180° fan) 400F, gas 6 and grease a 12 hole muffin tin with butter.

Beat the butter and sugar together until pale and fluffy, then beat in 2 of the eggs.

Fold in the flour and baking powder, mix thoroughly then fold in the blueberries.

Spoon the mixture into the prepared muffin pan. Beat the remaining egg, brush the tops of the muffins and scatter over the ground almonds.

Bake the muffins in the oven for 15-20 minutes or until the muffins are risen and golden brown. Allow them to cool for 5 minutes, then place them on a wire rack to cool completely.

Kiwi and pear smoothie

serves: 4

Ingredients:
6 kiwi fruit, peeled and chopped
½ honeydew melon,
peeled and chopped
2 pears, peeled,
cored and chopped
30 ml | 1 fl. oz lemon juice
6 ice cubes
icing (confectioners') sugar,
to taste

Method:
Place the pieces of kiwi fruit, honeydew melon and pear into a blender with the lemon juice and ice, and blend until smooth.

Add icing sugar to taste and serve. For added thickness, try adding natural yoghurt to the smoothie.

Berry pancakes

serves: 4

Ingredients:
150 g | 5 oz | 1 ½ cups plain
(all-purpose) flour
1 ½ tsp baking powder
½ tsp salt
30 g | 1 oz sugar
150 ml | 5 fl. oz | ⅔ cup milk
1 egg
30 g | 1 oz butter, melted
250 g | 9 oz | 2 cups raspberries,
strawberries and blueberries
maple syrup

Method:
Whisk the flour, baking powder, salt, sugar, milk, egg and the melted butter together. Beat the ingredients until you have a smooth, thick batter.

Melt a little unsalted butter in a large frying pan and drop ladles of batter into the pan, a few at a time.

When bubbles appear on the surface of the pancakes, turn them over and cook for 2-3 minutes, or until the pancakes have risen and are golden brown on both sides.

Repeat with the remaining batter, keeping the cooked pancakes warm. Serve with the mixed berries and maple syrup.

Eggs Benedict

serves: 4

Ingredients:
4 slices ham,
4 eggs
4 wholegrain toasts
90 ml | 3 fl. oz readymade
hollandaise sauce
chives, to garnish

Method:

Heat the grill and warm the ham. Set it aside in a warm place then grill the bacon until crisp.

Boil a saucepan of salted water, then turn the heat down to a very gentle simmer. Carefully break the eggs into the pan and poach for about 3-4 minutes.

Top the buttered toast with the ham, then remove the eggs from the pan with a slotted spoon and carefully place on top of the ham.

Spoon over the hollandaise sauce, add the bacon and season with salt and pepper and serve garnished with the chives.

Breakfast baguette

serves: 4

Ingredients:
45 ml | 1 ½ fl. oz vegetable oil
8 rashers bacon
8 sausages
30 ml | 1 fl. oz olive oil
200 g | 7 oz cherry tomatoes
4 eggs
1 tbsp chopped parsley
30 ml | 1 fl. oz butter
1 baguette, sliced in half
lengthways and toasted

Method:

Fry the bacon until lightly browned and crisp in a frying pan over a medium heat. Remove from the pan and set aside.

Add the oil to the pan and fry the sausages gently for about 15 minutes or until cooked through.

Meanwhile, heat the olive oil and gently cook the tomatoes in a small saucepan until the skins start to split.

Beat the eggs in a small bowl, season with salt and pepper and stir in the parsley. Heat the butter in a small pan and gently cook the eggs, stirring continuously, until they are cooked through but still soft.

Spoon the scrambled eggs onto the toasted baguette, top with the sausages and bacon and serve immediately with the tomatoes.

Boiled egg and toast soldiers

serves: 4

Ingredients:
8 eggs
8 slices white bread

Method:
Boil a pan of water over a medium heat and carefully place the eggs in the pan to cook for about 4 minutes.

While the eggs are cooking, toast the bread, spread with the butter, if desired, and cut into thin soldiers to dip into the soft boiled eggs.

Banana berry smoothies

serves: 4

Ingredients:
200 g | 7 oz strawberries
125 g | 4 ½ oz | 1 cup raspberries
2 bananas
250 ml | 9 fl. oz | 1 cup yoghurt
4 ice cubes

Method:
Set 4 strawberries aside to garnish and place the rest of them in a blender with the remaining ingredients.

Blend until smooth and serve garnished with the remaining strawberries.

Full English breakfast

serves: 4

Ingredients:
30 ml | 1 fl. oz oil
4 rashers bacon
8 sausages
30 g | 1 oz butter
100 g | 3 ½ oz mushrooms, sliced
4 tomatoes, halved
4 eggs
400 g | 14 oz | 2 cups baked beans
4 hash browns
4 slices bread, toasted

Method:
Heat the grill and add the bacon, hash browns and sausages, cooking for 15 minutes, turning to ensure they are evenly cooked on all sides.

While the bacon, hash browns and sausages are cooking, heat the butter in a small pan, over a medium heat, and gently cook the mushrooms until soft and season with salt and pepper.

Heat an oiled griddle pan on a high heat and cook the tomatoes, cut side down, until they start to soften, then remove from the pan and keep warm.

When the sausages and bacon are cooked, remove from the grill and keep them warm. Fry the eggs in the pan for 3-4 minutes and serve with the hot beans, bacon, sausages, hash browns and tomatoes.

French toast with berries

serves: 4

Ingredients:
3 eggs
125 ml | 4 ½ fl. oz | ½ cup milk
30 g | 1 oz sugar
30 g | 1 oz butter
6 slices white bread, or brioche
200 g | 7 oz | 2 cups mixed
frozen berries, thawed
icing (confectioners') sugar

Method:
Beat the eggs with the milk and the sugar.

Heat the butter in a frying pan until it is bubbling. Dip the bread into the egg mixture and fry in batches for 2-3 minutes on each side, or until golden brown.

Slice the bread in half diagonally and place on serving plates. Spoon over the mixed berries and dust with the icing sugar.

Pear and cinnamon yoghurt shake

serves: 4

Ingredients:
2 ripe pears, peeled, quartered,
cored and chopped
1 l | 35 fl. oz | 4 cups low-fat yoghurt
30 ml | 1 fl. oz honey
1 tsp ground cinnamon
a pinch of grated nutmeg

Method:
Put the pear, yoghurt, honey, cinnamon and nutmeg into a blender and whizz until smooth.

Pour the smoothie into glasses and sprinkle with a little cinnamon to serve.

Poached egg and smoked salmon

serves: 4

Ingredients:
4 eggs
2 English muffins, halved and toasted
30 g | 1 oz butter
1 handful baby spinach leaves
125 g | 4 ½ oz smoked salmon
45 g | 1 ½ oz sour cream, lightly whipped

Method:
Heat a wide pan of salted water to boiling point then turn the heat down and simmer. Carefully break the eggs into the pan and poach for 3-4 minutes.

Spread the muffins with butter, add the spinach leaves and smoked salmon then spoon over the sour cream.

Remove the eggs from the pan and place on top of the muffins. Season with salt and pepper and serve immediately.

Raspberry smoothie

serves: 4

Ingredients:
500 g | 18 oz | 4 cups raspberries
1 banana
200 ml | 7 fl. oz | ⅞ cup apple juice
4 ice cubes

Method:
Set aside 125 g of the raspberries and put the rest in a blender or food processor.

Add the remaining ingredients and blend until smooth. Serve garnished with the reserved raspberries.

Banana and date muffins

makes: 12

Ingredients:
2 bananas, very ripe
175 g | 6 oz | 1 cup dates, chopped
2 eggs
125 ml | 4 ½ fl. oz | ½ cup vegetable oil
175 g | 6 oz | ¾ cup sugar
1 tsp bicarbonate of soda (baking soda)
1 tsp vanilla extract
175 g | 6 oz | 1 ½ cups self-raising flour
icing (confectioners') sugar

Method:
Preheat the oven to 180°C (160° fan) 375F, gas 5 and butter a 12 hole muffin tin.

Mash the bananas in a large bowl and mix in the eggs and oil.

Add the sugar, bicarbonate of soda, vanilla, dates and flour and mix well until it has formed a smooth batter, then spoon into the muffin tin.

Bake the muffins for 15-20 minutes or until risen and golden brown. Serve dusted with icing sugar.

Porridge with berries

serves: 4

Ingredients:
175 g | 6 oz | 1 ½ cups porridge oats
500 ml | 18 fl. oz | 2 cups milk
500 ml | 18 fl. oz | 2 cups water
a pinch of salt
1 tbsp sugar
250 g | 9 oz | 2 cups mixed berries
250 ml | 9 fl. oz | 1 cup single cream

Method:
Place the oats, milk, water and salt in a pan and increase the heat to boiling point. Cook for 5-8 minutes, stirring continuously.

You may need to add a little more water or milk if the consistency is too thick. Stir in the sugar and serve in warmed bowls topped with berries and cream.

Bacon and maple syrup French toast

serves: 4

Ingredients:
12 slices bacon
4 eggs
150 ml | 5 fl. oz | ⅔ cup milk
1 tbsp sugar
2 tbsp butter
6 slices bread
maple syrup

Method:
Heat the grill and cook the bacon until crisp.

Meanwhile, whisk together the eggs, milk and sugar. Heat the butter in a large frying pan until it is bubbling. Dip the slices of bread in the mixture then fry in batches in the hot butter for about 2 minutes on each side or until golden brown.

Serve drizzled with the maple syrup and topped with the bacon.

Huevos rancheros

serves: 4

Ingredients:
45 ml | 1 ½ fl. oz vegetable oil
1 onion, finely chopped
1 clove of garlic, chopped
2 red chillies, finely chopped
1 red pepper, chopped
400 g | 14 oz | 2 cups tomatoes, canned
4 eggs

Method:
Heat the oil in a large pan over a medium heat and gently cook the onions until soft but not brown.

Add the garlic and chillies, cook for 2 minutes then add the pepper. Cook for 5 minutes then add the tomatoes, increase the heat to boiling point and simmer for 15 minutes. Season the pan to taste with salt and pepper.

Fry the eggs in a non-stick frying pan and serve on top of the pepper and tomato mixture.

Mango smoothie

serves: 4

Ingredients:
3 large, ripe mangoes
500 ml | 18 fl. oz | 2 cups milk, chilled
12 raspberries, frozen

Method:
Peel the mangoes and cut the flesh from the stone, reserving any juice.

Put the mango flesh and juice in a blender with the milk and blend until smooth.

Thread the raspberries onto 4 cocktail sticks and serve with the smoothies.

Blueberry pancakes

serves: 4

Ingredients:
150 g | 5 oz | 1 ½ cups plain
(all-purpose) flour
1 ½ tsp baking powder
½ tsp salt
30 g | 1 oz sugar
150 ml | 5 fl. oz | ⅔ cup milk
1 egg
45 g | 1 ½ oz butter, melted
blueberries
maple syrup

Method:
Whisk the flour, baking powder, salt, sugar, milk, egg and
the melted butter together. Beat the ingredients until you
have a smooth, thick batter.

Melt a little unsalted butter in a large frying pan, over a
medium to high heat, and drop ladles of batter into the pan,
a few at a time.

When bubbles appear on the surface of the pancakes,
turn them over and cook for 2-3 minutes or until the
pancakes have risen and are golden brown on both sides.

Repeat with the remaining batter, keeping the cooked
pancakes warm. Serve topped with the maple syrup
and blueberries.

Eggs Florentine

serves: 4

Ingredients:
2 large handfuls spinach
2 English muffins, halved and toasted
30 g | 1 oz butter
2 tomatoes, sliced
4 eggs
60 g | 2 oz hollandaise sauce

Method:

Heat the grill to its highest setting. Wash the spinach and place in a large pan. Cook for 2-3 minutes until wilted then drain well and squeeze out excess liquid.

Heat a wide pan of salted water to boiling point, then turn the heat down and simmer. Carefully break the eggs into the pan and poach for 3-4 minutes.

Spread the toasted muffins with butter, arrange the tomato slices on top and season with salt and pepper. Add the spinach.

Remove the eggs from the pan, drain well and place on top of the spinach.

Spoon over the hollandaise sauce, place under the grill for 2 minutes, then serve immediately.

brunch.

Brunch muffin

serves: 4

Ingredients:
4 eggs
1 tbsp oil
4 slices bacon
4 large mushrooms
4 English muffins, halved and toasted
baby spinach leaves

Method:
Half fill a large saucepan with water and heat it to simmering point. Carefully drop in the eggs and poach gently for about 3-4 minutes.

Heat the oil in a frying pan and cook the bacon until crispy. Remove the bacon from the pan and keep warm. Add the mushrooms to the pan and cook for 5 minutes until tender.

Butter the toasted muffins. Place the spinach leaves on each muffin and top with a poached egg, a mushroom and the bacon.

Piperade eggs with ham

serves: 4

Ingredients:
30 ml | 1 fl. oz olive oil
1 onion, finely chopped
2 red peppers, chopped
2 plum tomatoes, diced
4 slices ham
30 g | 1 oz butter
6 eggs, beaten
4 slices bread, toasted

Method:
Heat the oil in a pan and gently fry the onion until soft but not brown. Add the peppers and tomatoes and continue cooking, stirring from time to time.

Heat the grill to its highest setting and grill the ham until lightly browned. Set it aside and keep warm.

Heat the butter in a small pan and add the eggs. Cook until scrambled then season with salt and pepper and remove the pan from the heat.

When the peppers are tender, stir in the scrambled eggs and spoon the piperade into serving dishes. Serve with the toasted bread and the grilled ham.

Chicken Caesar salad

serves: 4

Ingredients:
45 ml | 1 ½ fl. oz oil
2 slices white bread, cut into cubes
2 large chicken breasts, skinned
1 Kos lettuce, roughly torn
12 cherry tomatoes, halved
½ cucumber, peeled and sliced
Parmesan cheese, to serve
Caesar salad dressing, to serve

Method:
Heat the oil in a frying pan and fry the cubes of bread, stirring frequently, until golden brown and crispy on all sides. Remove the bread from the pan, drain on kitchen paper and set aside.

Heat 1-2 tablespoons of oil in a griddle pan. Flatten the chicken breasts with a meat hammer or rolling pin, season with salt and pepper and grill in the pan for 3-4 minutes on each side or until cooked through.

Place the lettuce, tomatoes and sliced cucumber in serving bowls. Slice the chicken and add to the salad. Scatter over the bread croutons and Parmesan shavings and serve with the dressing alongside.

Apple crumble muffins

makes: 12

Ingredients:
225 g | 8 oz | 2 cups plain
(all-purpose) flour
2 tsp baking powder
75 g | 2 ½ oz | ½ cup brown sugar
1 tsp mixed spice
2 apples, cored and chopped
1 egg
150 ml | 5 fl. oz | ⅔ cup sour cream
50 g | 2 oz | ¼ cup butter, melted

For the topping:
30 g | 1 oz butter
1 tbsp flour
30 g | 1 oz demerara sugar
30 g | 1 oz ground almonds
60 g | 2 oz sunflower seeds

Method:
For the crumble topping, rub the butter into the flour, sugar and almonds until the mixture resembles breadcrumbs. Stir in the sunflower seeds and set aside.

Heat the oven to 190°C (170° fan) 375F, gas 5 and line a 12 hole muffin tin with large paper cases.

For the muffins, sift the flour and baking powder into a mixing bowl. Stir in the sugar, mixed spice and apples.

Mix the egg, soured cream and melted butter together. Pour the wet ingredients into the dry and stir lightly until everything is just combined. The mixture will be lumpy.

Spoon the mixture into the paper cases, sprinkle over the topping and bake for 15 minutes or until the muffins are risen and firm. Place them on a wire rack to cool completely.

Croissants with summer berries

serves: 4

Ingredients:
4 croissants
375 g | 13 oz | 3 cups raspberries,
strawberries, blackcurrants and
blueberries
60 ml | 2 fl. oz yoghurt
60 ml | 2 fl. oz runny honey

Method:
Heat the oven to 200°C (180° fan) 400F, gas 6.

Place the croissants in an ovenproof and heat in
the oven for 5 minutes.

Split the croissants in half horizontally.

Mix the yoghurt, honey and berries together and
spoon onto the croissants.

Tomato frittata

serves: 4

Ingredients:
45 ml | 1 ½ fl. oz oil
1 onion, finely chopped
6 eggs, beaten
4 tomatoes, chopped
1 tbsp chopped parsley

Method:
Heat the oil in a 26 cm / 10 " frying pan and gently cook the onion, until soft, for 10 minutes. Heat the grill to its highest setting.

Season the eggs with salt and pepper and mix with the parsley and pour into the pan. Stir gently then add half of the tomatoes and leave to cook until the eggs are nearly set.

Place the pan under the grill until the eggs are golden brown and cooked through. Serve topped with the remaining tomatoes.

Avocado and bean salad

serves: 4

Ingredients:
45 ml | 1 ½ fl. oz olive oil
1 lime, juiced
1 clove of garlic, finely chopped
2 cans red kidney beans,
drained and rinsed
2 avocados, peeled,
stone removed and chopped
2 shallots, finely chopped
salad cress

Method:
Mix the oil, lime juice and garlic together and season the dressing with salt and pepper to make a dressing.

Mix the kidney beans, avocados, shallots and salad cress together, spoon into bowls and drizzle over the dressing.

Chicken and pepper quesadillas

serves: 4

Ingredients:
90 ml | 3 fl. oz vegetable oil
2 cloves of garlic, chopped
1 red chilli, finely chopped
2 red peppers, sliced
2 green peppers, sliced
8 flour tortillas
200 g | 7 oz | 2 cups grated cheese
450 g | 1 lb cooked chicken, shredded

Method:
Heat 4 tablespoons of the oil in a large pan and gently cook the garlic and chilli until soft.

Add the peppers, season with salt and pepper and cook gently for 10 minutes.

Meanwhile, heat a little oil in a large frying pan and cook the flour tortillas on one side only until they start to puff up. Set aside and keep warm.

When the peppers are cooked, add a little more oil to the frying pan, lay one tortilla, uncooked side down in the pan, scatter over some cheese, peppers and chicken and fold over. Cook until the cheese starts to melt then remove from the pan and keep warm.

Repeat with the remaining tortillas and serve immediately.

Potato and green bean salad

serves: 4

Ingredients:
300 g | 10 oz small new
potatoes, scrubbed
2 handfuls green
(string) beans, trimmed
45 ml | 1 ½ fl. oz olive oil
1 tbsp white wine vinegar
2 red onions, sliced
250 g | 9 oz cherry tomatoes, halved
60 g | 2 oz capers, drained
1 small bunch basil

Method:
Cook the potatoes in large pan of boiling, salted water for 10-15 minutes until they are tender.

Blanch the beans in boiling water for 3 minutes. Drain them and refresh under cold running water.

Mix the oil and vinegar together and season with salt and pepper to make the dressing.

When the potatoes are cooked, drain well, refresh under cold water and cut the potatoes into quarters.

Mix the potatoes, beans, onions, tomatoes and capers with the dressing in a large bowl. Roughly tear the basil leaves and mix with the salad.

Mushroom and bacon croissants

serves: 4

Ingredients:
8 rashers bacon
4 croissants
30 g | 1 oz butter
250 g | 9 oz mixed mushrooms
60 ml | 2 fl. oz single cream

Method:

Heat the grill to its highest setting and grill the bacon until crisp.

Heat the butter in a small pan and gently cook the mushrooms over a low heat until they start to soften. Add the cream, season with salt and pepper and cook for 5 minutes.

When the bacon is cooked, set it aside and place the croissants under the grill for 2 minutes until warmed through.

Slice open the croissants horizontally, fill with the mushroom mixture and top with the bacon.

Oven-baked eggs

serves: 4

Ingredients:
6 eggs
30 ml | 1 fl. oz olive oil
2 tbsp mixed herbs, chopped
1 tsp mustard powder
60 g | 2 oz crème fraiche
1 tbsp butter, melted
mixed salad leaves, to serve

Method:
Place the eggs in a pan of salted water and increase the heat to boiling point. Leave to simmer for 5 minutes then peel very carefully, slice in half and remove the yolks with a teaspoon and place them in a small bowl. Heat the oven to 200°C (180° fan) 400F, gas 6.

Place the oil and herbs in a small pan with the herbs, heat very gently then set aside. Mash the egg yolks with the mustard powder, crème fraiche and melted butter until smooth. Season with salt and pepper.

Fill the cavity of the egg whites with the egg yolk mixture, place in a small roasting pan and bake in the oven for 5 minutes.

Serve the eggs on a bed of salad leaves with the herb oil drizzled over.

Scrambled eggs and chives on toast

serves: 4

Ingredients:
45 g | 1 ½ oz butter
4 slices white bread
6 eggs
fresh chives, chopped

Method:
Toast the bread under the grill and keep it warm.

Melt the butter in a small frying pan over a low heat.
Beat the eggs, season with salt and pepper and pour into
the pan. Cook very gently, stirring all the time, until the
eggs are just cooked.

Serve the eggs on the toast garnished with the and chives.

Avocado tostadas

serves: 4

Ingredients:
30 g | 1 oz sesame seeds
2 ripe avocados, peeled,
stone removed and diced
6 medium tomatillos (green tomatoes),
peeled and chopped
1 green chilli, finely chopped
2 limes, juiced
60 ml | 2 fl. oz vegetable oil
4 tostadas
sea salt

Method:
Toast the sesame seeds in a dry pan and set aside.

Mix together the chopped avocados, tomatillos, chilli,
lime juice and oil.

Bake or fry the tostadas according to packet instructions,
spoon over the salsa and serve sprinkled with the toasted
sesame seeds and salt.

Potato and chorizo tortilla

serves: 4

Ingredients:
45 ml | 1 ½ fl. oz oil
2 onions, finely sliced
6 eggs
2 medium potatoes, cooked,
peeled and sliced
1 cooked chorizo, sliced

Method:

Heat the oil in a frying pan about 26 cm / 10 " in diameter and fry the onions for 5-10 minutes until they are browned and starting to caramelise.

Heat the grill to its highest setting. Beat the eggs in a large bowl and season with salt and pepper. Carefully mix in the sliced potato, add the fried onions and pour the mixture back into the pan.

Add the sliced chorizo to the pan, cook until the eggs are nearly set, then set the pan under the grill until golden brown and the eggs are cooked though.

French toast sandwich

serves: 4

Ingredients:
1 tbsp oil
4 slices ham
4 tomatoes, sliced
30 g | 1 oz butter
4 eggs
200 ml | 7 fl. oz | 1 cup milk
8 slices white bread
1 bunch watercress,
washed and chopped

Method:

Heat the oil in a frying pan and fry the bacon until lightly browned. Remove from the heat and set aside.

Fry the tomatoes until soft, then remove from the pan and set aside. Wipe the pan clean with kitchen paper and add the butter. Heat gently until it starts to bubble.

Beat the eggs and milk together and season with salt and pepper. Dip the bread in the egg mixture then fry gently in batches for 2 minutes on each side until golden brown.

Make the sandwiches with the ham, tomatoes and watercress, garnish with the remaining watercress and serve immediately.

Chicken wraps

serves: 4

Ingredients:
45 ml | 1 ½ fl. oz olive oil
2 chicken breasts, skinned and sliced
8 flour tortillas
1 red pepper, sliced
1 green pepper, sliced
2 carrots, sliced
2 tomatoes, peeled and sliced
1 lemon, juiced

Method:
Heat the oven to 200°C (180° fan), 400F, gas 6.

Heat the oil in a frying pan. Season the chicken with salt and pepper and fry for 5 minutes, stirring occasionally, until the chicken is cooked through. Set aside.

Warm the tortillas in the oven for a few minutes. Remove from the oven and top them with the chicken and vegetables, sprinkle over the lemon juice and roll up, tucking in the sides.

Slice the wraps in half and garnish with parsley.

Spicy chicken salad

serves: 4

Ingredients:
30 ml | 1 fl. oz vegetable oil
1 tsp curry powder
1 chilli, finely chopped
2 large chicken breasts,
skinned and cut into large chunks
45 ml | 1 ½ fl. oz sesame oil
1 lime, juiced
1 tbsp fish sauce
1 tsp sugar
1 tbsp chopped coriander (cilantro)
1 can pineapple chunks, drained
1 papaya, peeled and cut into chunks
8 asparagus spears
2 handfuls mixed salad leaves
1 courgette (zucchini),
thinly sliced lengthways
1 lemon, cut into wedges

Method:

Heat the oil in a large pan over a medium heat and add the curry powder and chilli. Cook for a minute then add the chicken and cook for 10 minutes until browned. Add the asparagus and cook for a further 3 minutes.

Mix the sesame oil, lime juice, fish sauce, sugar and coriander together to make a dressing.

Pour the contents of the pan in a bowl with the pineapple, papaya and the dressing.

Place the salad leaves in bowls, add the chicken mixture and garnish with the curled courgette strips and lemon wedges.

Homemade muesli bars

makes: 12

Ingredients:
110 g | 4 oz | 1 cup rolled oats
175 g | 6 oz | ¾ cup butter
120 ml | 4 ½ fl. oz honey
45 g | 1 ½ oz brown sugar
100 g | 3 ½ oz | ⅔ cup
hazelnuts (cobnuts), chopped
100 g | 3 ½ oz | ⅔ cup
Brazil nuts, chopped
100 g | 3 ½ oz | ⅔ cup
cashew nuts, chopped
150 g | 5 oz | 1 cup figs, chopped
150 g | 5 oz | 1 cup prunes, chopped
50 g | 1 ¾ oz | ½ cup pumpkin seeds
125 g | 4 ½ oz | 1 cup sesame seeds

Method:
Grease a 20 cm x 20 cm / 8 " x 8 " roasting tin and line it with greaseproof paper. Toast the oats in a large frying pan over a low heat until lightly browned. Remove the oats from the pan and set aside.

Heat the butter, honey and sugar in the pan, until the butter has melted and the sugar has dissolved.

Return the oats to the pan and add the remaining ingredients. Mix well and pour into the lined roasting tin. Press the mixture down and let it cool, then slice into bars.

Croque madame

serves: 4

Ingredients:
8 slices wholemeal bread
30 g | 1 oz butter
4 eggs, beaten
4 slices blue cheese
2 large tomatoes, sliced
4 slices Parma ham
chopped chives, to garnish

Method:
Heat the grill to a high setting and toast 4 slices of bread on each side. Set aside and keep warm.

Melt the butter in a small frying pan and gently cook the eggs until they are just set, stirring all the time. Season with salt and pepper and remove the pan from the heat.

Toast the remaining 4 slices of bread on one side, turn over and lay on the slices of blue cheese. Return to the grill until the cheese has started to melt.

Lay the tomato slices on top of the cheese, add the ham and the remaining slices of toasted bread, then top with the scrambled eggs and garnish with the chopped chives and a little black pepper.

Bruschetta

serves: 4

Ingredients:
30 ml | 1 fl. oz olive oil
2 shallots, finely sliced
6 plum tomatoes, halved lengthways
sliced baguette, toasted
2 cloves of garlic, 1 finely chopped
1 handful rocket (arugula)

Method:

Heat the oil in a small frying pan over a medium heat and cook the shallots and the chopped garlic until lightly browned.

Add the tomatoes, cut side down, and cook gently for 3 minutes.

Rub the whole garlic clove over the toasted bread, top with the rocket, shallots and tomatoes and season with salt and pepper.

lunch.

Prawn and avocado salad

serves: 4

Ingredients:
100 g | 3 ½ oz green (string) beans
2 avocados, peeled,
stoned removed and chopped
1 tbsp lemon juice
100 g | 3 ½ oz mixed lettuce leaves,
washed and roughly torn
1 handful baby spinach
75 g | 2 ½ oz button mushrooms, sliced
12 cherry tomatoes
1 red pepper, cut into fine strips
1 small beetroot, peeled and
cut into fine strips
250 g | 9 oz cooked prawns
(shrimps), peeled
60 g | 2 oz Marie Rose sauce

Method:
In a small frying pan, cook the mushrooms for 5 minutes, over a medium heat, until soft.

Blanch the beans in boiling water for 3 minutes, drain, refresh under cold water and pat dry. Slice the beans into smaller, bite-size pieces.

Mix the avocado with the lemon juice, salt and pepper, to prevent it from becoming brown.

Add the lettuce, spinach, mushrooms, tomatoes, pepper, beetroot, prawns and beans to the avocado and drizzle over the dressing and serve.

Grilled seafood kebabs

serves: 4-6

Ingredients:
4 rashers bacon
8 king prawns, peeled
12 scallops
1 lemon, cut into quarters
16 prawns (shrimp)
2 limes, sliced
60 ml | 2 fl. oz olive oil
1 red chilli, finely chopped
coriander (cilantro) leaves, chopped
lemon oil and soy sauce

Method:
Cut each bacon rasher in half.

Wrap the king prawns in the bacon and thread onto 4 wooden skewers, alternating with the scallops. Finish with a lemon quarter at the end of each skewer.

Thread the prawns onto 4 more skewers, alternating with the lime slices.

Heat the grill to a high heat, heat a griddle pan until very hot or cook the skewers on the barbeque. Mix the olive oil with the chilli, season with salt and pepper and brush over the skewers.

Cook the skewers for about 4 minutes each side or until the prawns are cooked through and garnish with the coriander, lemon oil and soy sauce alongside for dipping.

Serve with fresh salad and crusty bread.

lunch.

Caprese sandwich

serves: 4

Ingredients:
8 slices sourdough, toasted
60 ml | 2 fl. oz olive oil
200 g | 7 oz buffalo mozzarella,
roughly crumbled
2 large ripe beef tomatoes, sliced
4 yellow tomatoes, sliced
4 sprigs lambs lettuce
2 sprigs basil, leaves only

Method:
Place one slice of toasted bread on each of 4 plates.

Drizzle over a little oil then layer over the mozzarella and the tomatoes, drizzling more oil and season generously with salt and pepper.

Finish with a layer of lambs lettuce and basil leaves and top with the remaining slices of toast.

Pasta with walnut pesto

serves: 4

Ingredients:
400 g | 14 oz tagliatelle
125 g | 5 oz | 1 ¼ cups walnuts
1 handful basil, chopped
2 cloves of garlic, chopped
110 ml | 4 fl. oz olive oil
1 tbsp lemon juice
30 ml | 1 fl. oz vegetable oil
200 g | 7 oz cherry tomatoes
100 g | 3 ½ oz Roquefort, crumbled

Method:

Heat a large pan of salted water to the boil and cook the pasta according to packet instructions.

To make the pesto, place 100 g of the walnuts, basil, garlic and olive oil in a blender or food processor and pulse until it forms a coarse paste. Season the pesto with salt, pepper and the lemon juice and set it aside.

Heat the vegetable oil in a small pan and gently cook the tomatoes until the skins blister.

When the pasta is cooked, drain well and mix in the pesto and cooked tomatoes. Sprinkle over the Roquefort and remaining walnuts and serve immediately.

Lamb pittas with hummus and mint

serves: 4

Ingredients:
1 tbsp cumin seeds
1 tbsp sesame seeds
60 ml | 2 fl. oz oil
1 onion, finely chopped
1 clove of garlic, finely chopped
600 g | 1 ¼ lbs minced (ground) lamb
2 tbsp mint, chopped
1 egg
8 pitta breads, warmed in the oven
110 g | 4 oz hummus
mint leaves, to garnish

Method:
Toast the cumin and sesame seeds in a large, dry frying pan for 30 seconds then set them aside.

Heat 2 tablespoons of the oil in the pan and gently fry the onion and garlic over a low heat until soft.

Place the lamb in a large bowl and add the cooked onion and garlic, mint and the egg. Reserve a few of the toasted seeds for the garnish and add the rest to the meat mixture. Season the lamb with salt and pepper and mix well with your hands then shape into 8 patties.

Wipe the pan clean with kitchen paper then heat the remaining oil and fry the meat patties for 4-5 minutes on each side, or until cooked through.

Spread the pitta breads with hummus, and serve the burgers in the warm pitta breads, sprinkled with the remaining toasted seeds.

Warm chorizo and potato salad

serves: 4

Ingredients:
600 g | 1 ½ lbs new potatoes, cooked
30 ml | 1 fl. oz olive oil
400 g | 14 oz chorizo sausage,
thinly sliced
1 radicchio, torn
30 ml | 1 fl. oz white wine vinegar
4 tbsp of chives, cress, oregano, basil
salt and ground black pepper

Method:
Cut the cooked potatoes into thick slices.

Heat the oil in a pan over a medium heat and fry the potatoes until golden brown, remove them from the pan and set aside. Fry the chorizo until the fat begins to run.

Place the radicchio in a bowl and add the potatoes and chorizo. Add a little water to the liquid in the pan, stir in the vinegar and the herbs and season with salt and ground black pepper to taste, let it bubble and then pour over the salad.

Fish soup

serves: 4

Ingredients:
45 ml | 1 ½ fl. oz oil
1 onion, finely chopped
2 cloves of garlic, chopped
30 ml | 1 fl. oz dry vermouth
1 l | 35 fl. oz | 4 cups fish
or vegetable stock
4 large tomatoes
150 g | 5 oz | 1 ½ cups pasta
1 medium courgette (zucchini),
chopped
450 g | 1 lb cod fillet,
cut into large chunks
30 ml | 1 fl. oz lemon juice
basil leaves, to garnish

Method:
Heat the oil in a large pan and gently cook the onion and garlic until soft but not brown. Add the vermouth, let it bubble, then add the stock. Increase the heat to boiling point and then simmer for 5 minutes.

Drop the tomatoes into boiling water for 30 seconds, refresh them in cold water, then peel and slice into small pieces and remove the seeds. Add the tomatoes to the pan.

Add the pasta, increase the heat to boiling point and then simmer for 5 minutes.

Add the courgette and the fish, simmer for 5 minutes until the pasta is tender and the fish is cooked through.

Season with salt, pepper and lemon juice, garnish with basil and serve.

American club sandwich

serves: 4

Ingredients:
12 slices seeded loaf
8 rashers bacon
30 g | 1 oz butter
2 large chicken breasts, skinned
1 tsp dried mixed herbs
200 g | 7 oz canned sweetcorn
(corn kernels)
small bunch rocket (arugula)
1 red onion, finely sliced into rings
90 g | 3 oz mayonnaise
30 ml | 2 fl. oz lime juice

Method:

Heat a grill and toast the bread on both sides. Set it aside and keep warm. Flatten the chicken breasts with a meat hammer or rolling pin, seasoning it with salt and pepper.

Grill the bacon in the griddle pan until browned then set it aside and keep warm.

Melt the butter in the pan and cook the chicken breasts for 3 minutes on each side. Add the herbs to the pan and baste the meat with the juices. Mix the lime juice and mayonnaise together and spread on the toast.

To assemble the sandwich, slice each chicken breast in half. Lay one piece of chicken on a slice of toasted bread, spoon over some sweetcorn, add another slice of bread then the bacon, rocket, onion and finally another slice of bread. Secure with cocktail sticks and serve immediately.

Salad nicoise

serves: 4

Ingredients:
4 eggs
8 lettuce leaves, roughly torn
1 red onion, thinly sliced
4 tomatoes, roughly chopped
1 can butterbeans, drained and rinsed
2 cans tuna, drained
4 sundried tomatoes, roughly chopped
45 ml | 1 ½ fl. oz olive oil
1 tbsp white wine vinegar
1 clove of garlic, finely chopped
1 tbsp parsley, chopped

Method:

Put the eggs in a pan of water and increase the heat to boiling point. Simmer for 4 minutes then rinse them under running water and peel off the shells and cut the eggs into quarters.

Arrange the lettuce, onion, tomatoes, butterbeans, tuna and sundried tomatoes into lunch boxes or plates and add the eggs.

Mix the oil, vinegar and garlic together to make a dressing and drizzle over the salad. Season with salt and freshly ground black pepper and garnish with the chopped parsley.

Pita bread pizzas

serves: 4

Ingredients:
60 ml | 2 fl. oz olive oil
2 aubergines (eggplants), sliced
250 ml | 9 fl. oz | 1 cup
readymade tomato sauce
2 tsp dried oregano
12 cherry tomatoes, halved
250 g | 9 oz | 2 cups feta
cheese, cubed
1 tsp fresh oregano
50 g | 2 oz Cheddar cheese

Method:
Heat the oven to 220°C (200° fan) 425F, gas 7.

Heat the oil in a large frying pan and fry the aubergine slices until they are starting to brown. Season them with salt and pepper and add a little more oil during cooking if needed.

Place the pita breads on an oiled baking tray and spread with the tomato sauce. Sprinkle over the dried oregano and season with salt and pepper.

Lay the fried aubergine slices and halved tomatoes on top of the sauce, followed by the Cheddar cheese, and bake in the oven for 10 minutes.

Scatter over the feta cheese and oregano and serve.

Grilled vegetable English muffins

serves: 4

Ingredients:
4 tomatoes, cut into thick slices
1 courgette (zucchini), sliced
2 red onions, cut into wedges
1 red pepper, cut into large chunks
45 ml | 1 ½ fl. oz olive oil
1 tsp dried mixed herbs
4 English muffins, cut in half
parsley, to garnish

Method:
Preheat the grill to a high heat.

Mix all the vegetables together on a baking sheet. Drizzle with the oil and season with salt and ground black pepper.

Grill for 10 minutes, sprinkle with herbs, then carefully turn the vegetables over and continue to grill for 4 minutes.

Toast the muffins under the grill and then top the muffin halves with the vegetables and garnish with parsley.

Beef fajitas

serves: 4

Ingredients:
30 ml | 1 fl. oz vegetable oil
450 g | 1 lb beef fillet
2 ripe avocados
200 ml | 7 fl. oz | 1 cup crème fraiche
1 lime, juiced
2 tbsp chopped coriander (cilantro)
4 flour tortillas

To serve:
tomato salsa
shredded lettuce
sour cream

Method:

Heat the oven to 220°C (200° fan) 425F, gas 7.

Heat the oil in an ovenproof frying pan. Season the beef with salt and pepper and sear on all sides until browned. Transfer the pan to the oven and cook for 15-20 minutes.

Mash the avocados with the crème fraiche, lime juice and chopped coriander. Season with salt and pepper and set aside.

When the beef is cooked, remove from the oven and leave to rest for 5 minutes. Place the tortillas in the oven to heat gently.

Slice the meat and fill the tortillas with meat slices, avocado cream, tomato salsa, shredded lettuce and sour cream.

Garlic prawn spaghetti

serves: 4

Ingredients:
400 g | 14 oz spaghetti
small bunch coriander
(cilantro), chopped
30 ml | 1 fl. oz oil
small piece fresh ginger,
peeled and finely chopped
2 cloves of garlic, finely chopped
4 spring onions (scallions), finely sliced
450 g | 1 lb prawns (shrimps), shelled
300 g | 11 oz | 2 cups frozen
peas, thawed
125 ml | 4 ½ fl. oz | ½ cup fish stock
30 ml | 1 fl. oz lemon juice

Method:
Cook the spaghetti according to the packet instructions. When it is cooked, drain well and refresh under cold running water. Reserve a few sprigs of coriander for the garnish, then finely chop the rest.

Heat the oil in a large pan. Add the ginger and garlic, fry for 2 minutes and then add the spring onions. Stir fry for 2 minutes then add the prawns, stir fry for 1 minute then add the peas and the fish stock.

Season with salt, pepper and lemon juice and stir in the cooked spaghetti and the chopped coriander. Heat through, garnish with coriander and serve.

Mini pizzas

serves: 4

Ingredients:
8 mini pizza bases
60 g | 2 oz tomato puree
2 tsp dried oregano
250 g | 9 oz | 2 cups feta
cheese, cubed
150 g | 5 oz | 1 ½ cups
pitted black olives, sliced
1 tbsp olive oil
fresh oregano leaves, to garnish

Method:

Heat the oven to 220°C (200° fan) 425F, gas 7.

Spread the pizza bases with the tomato puree and scatter over a little dried oregano. Scatter over the feta cheese and olives and drizzle with a little olive oil.

Place on a greased baking tray and bake in the oven for 10-15 minutes, until the pizza bases are golden brown.

Garnish with oregano leaves and serve.

Roast chicken with almond rice

serves: 4

Ingredients:
30 ml | 1 fl. oz oil
1 onion, finely chopped
1 tsp turmeric
1 tsp ground cumin
1 tsp salt
1 tsp curry powder
200 g | 7 oz | 1 cup basmati rice
750 ml | 26 fl. oz | 3 cups
vegetable stock
30 g | 1 oz butter
4 large chicken breasts
2 tbsp parsley, chopped
75 g | 2 ½ oz | 1 cup flaked
(slivered) almonds

Method:
Heat the oil in a large pan and cook the onion for 2 minutes. Add the turmeric, cumin, salt and curry powder, stir for 1 minute then add the rice.

Stir to coat the rice with the oil then pour on the stock, increase the heat to boiling point and then simmer for 20 minutes, or until the rice is cooked. You may need to add a little water during the cooking.

Flatten the chicken breasts with a meat hammer or a rolling pin. Heat the butter in a large frying pan and cook the chicken breasts over a medium heat for 3-4 minutes on each side, basting with the butter. Add the chopped parsley to the pan and baste once more.

Stir the almonds into the cooked rice. Slice each chicken breast in half and serve them on the rice with a little more parsley scattered over.

Parma ham and dandelion salad

serves: 4

Ingredients:
4 eggs
60 ml | 2 fl. oz olive oil
1 tbsp Dijon mustard
1 tbsp red wine vinegar
a pinch of sugar
30 g | 1 oz pine nuts
50 g | 2 oz young dandelion leaves
100 | 3 ½ oz mixed lettuce leaves,
roughly torn
8 slices Parma ham, chopped
4 sprigs watercress, chopped

Method:
Place the eggs in a small pan of water, increase the heat to boiling point and simmer for 4-6 minutes.

Mix the olive oil, mustard, vinegar and sugar together to make a dressing. Season with salt and pepper and set it aside.

Toast the pine nuts in a dry pan for about 30 seconds or until golden brown, stirring all the time.

When the eggs are done, rinse them under cold running water and carefully peel off the shells.

Arrange the dandelion leaves, lettuce and Parma ham on serving plates. Cut the eggs in half and add to the plate.

Drizzle the salad leaves with the dressing and garnish with the watercress.

Baked potato with bacon filling

serves: 4

Ingredients:
4 baking potatoes
30 ml | 1 fl. oz oil
1 shallot, finely chopped
1 clove of garlic, finely chopped
8 rashers bacon, chopped
2 tomatoes, deseeded and chopped
60 g | 2 oz butter
150 g | 5 oz | 1 ½ cups grated cheese

Method:
Prick the potatoes with a fork and rub with a little oil. Cook in the microwave for 5-6 minutes, or according to the microwave instructions. Repeat the cooking time as necessary.

Meanwhile, heat the remaining oil in a pan and fry the shallot, garlic and bacon until the bacon is browned and crisp.

Add the chopped tomatoes and cook for 2 minutes. Slice the cooked potatoes open, add a little butter then add the cheese and top with the bacon mixture.

Add the remaining butter, sprinkle with salt and pepper and serve immediately.

Oven-roasted salmon

serves: 4

Ingredients:
800 g | 1 ¾ lbs new potatoes,
scrubbed and halved
4 salmon fillets
45 ml | 1 ½ fl. oz olive oil
50 g | 2 oz fruit mustard
45 ml | 1 ½ fl. oz white wine
2 courgettes (zucchini), cut into batons

Method:
Heat the oven to 200°C (180° fan) 400F, gas 6.

Place the potatoes in a large pan of salted water and boil for 10 minutes until nearly tender.

Rub the salmon pieces with a little olive oil and place them skin side down in a greased roasting pan. Put a teaspoon of the fruit mustard onto each piece of fish, pour the wine into the pan, cover with tin foil and place in the oven for 15 minutes, or until the fish is just cooked through.

When the potatoes are nearly cooked, add the courgettes and boil until they are tender. Drain well and mix in the remaining olive oil and season with salt and pepper.

Serve the fish with the vegetables, spoon over the remaining fruit mustard and serve.

Chicken satay with chilli dip

serves: 4

Ingredients:
For the satay:
2 chicken breasts, skinned
90 g | 3 oz smooth peanut butter
1 tsp turmeric
125 ml | 4 ½ fl. oz | ½ cup
light soy sauce
1 red chilli, finely chopped

For the dipping sauce:
45 ml | 1 ½ fl. oz fish sauce
30 ml | 1 fl. oz light soy sauce
1 lime, juiced
1 tsp sugar
2 red chillies, sliced

Method:
Flatten the chicken breasts with a meat hammer or rolling pin and cut each one into strips.

Mix the peanut butter, turmeric, soy sauce and chilli together and season with salt and pepper.

Mix the chicken strips with the satay sauce and set it aside for 10 minutes.

To make dipping sauce, mix the ingredients together and set aside.

Heat the grill, thread the chicken strips onto wooden skewers and grill for about 5 minutes, turning frequently.

Serve the satay skewers with the dipping sauce as a light snack, or serve with salad and potatoes as a main meal.

Grilled courgette and goat's cheese salad

serves: 4

Ingredients:
60 ml | 2 fl. oz olive oil
2 cloves of garlic, chopped
2 sprigs of thyme, chopped
1 lemon, juiced
2 courgettes (zucchini), sliced
300 g | 11 oz | 2 cups chickpeas (garbanzos)
2 handfuls baby spinach
1 bunch mint
200 g | 7 oz | 2 cups goat's cheese

Method:
Mix the olive oil with the thyme, garlic and lemon juice. Pour over the courgettes and marinate for about 10 minutes.

Heat a lightly oiled griddle pan and cook the courgettes for about 6-8 minutes, turning frequently and season with salt and pepper.

Drain the chicken peas and rinse under running water. Wash and trim the spinach and the mint, then shake dry.

Mix the spinach with the mint and chickpeas, add the courgettes and sprinkle over the crumbled goat's cheese.

Salmon fillet with green beans

serves: 4

Ingredients:
45 ml | 1 ½ fl. oz oil
1 red pepper, deseeded and sliced
250 g | 9 oz green (string) beans
30 g | 1 oz butter
150 | 5 oz salmon fillets x 4
1 tbsp capers
tarragon leaves, to serve

Method:
Heat the oil in a frying pan and gently cook the peppers until softened.

Cook the beans in a pan of boiling, salted water for 5 minutes. Drain well and set aside. Remove the cooked peppers from the pan, wipe it clean and add the butter. When it is bubbling, add the salmon and cook for 3-4 minutes, skin side down, then turn it over and cook for a further 3-4 minutes.

Place the green beans onto serving plates with the salmon on top. Garnish with pepper strips and scatter over the capers and tarragon leaves.

Quinoa with butternut squash

serves: 4

Ingredients:
oil
1 onion, finely chopped
1 clove of garlic, chopped
600 g | 1 ¼ lbs butternut squash, peeled, deseeded and chopped
300 g | 11 oz | 1 ½ cups quinoa, washed
750 ml | 26 fl. oz | 3 cups vegetable stock
60 g | 2 oz pomegranate seeds
2 tbsp parsley, chopped

Method:

Heat the oil in a large saucepan and gently cook the onion and garlic over a low heat until soft.

Add the squash, fry briefly over a high heat then add the quinoa and the stock.

Increase the heat to boiling point, then reduce the heat and simmer for 15-20 minutes or until the quinoa is cooked and the squash is tender. Add a little more stock or water during cooking if needed. Season then pan with salt and pepper and stir in the parsley.

Scatter the pomegranate seeds over the dish and serve.

Spicy chicken with green beans

serves: 4

Ingredients:
4 chicken breasts, skinned
60 ml | 2 fl. oz olive oil
2 cloves of garlic, chopped
1 red chilli, chopped
1 tsp coriander seeds, lightly crushed
1 tsp ground cumin
2 tbsp coriander (cilantro), chopped
1 lemon, juiced
green (string) beans, to serve

Method:
Flatten the chicken breasts with a meat hammer or rolling pin.

Mix the oil, garlic, chilli, coriander seeds, cumin, coriander and lemon juice together. Season with salt and pepper and rub the marinade into the chicken breasts.

Leave the chicken to marinate while the beans steam for 5 minutes, then set them aside in a warm place.

Heat a little oil in a large frying pan and fry the chicken breasts for 2 minutes on each side over a medium heat, then add the marinade and cook for 3-4 more minutes, basting from time to time, or until the chicken is cooked through.

Serve with the green beans and new potatoes.

Goat's cheese wrapped in bacon

serves: 4

Ingredients:
30 ml | 1 fl. oz red wine vinegar
1 tbsp balsamic vinegar
30 ml | 1 fl. oz orange juice
45 ml | 1 ½ fl. oz olive oil
8 rashers bacon, thinly sliced
250 g | 9 oz goat's cheese,
thickly sliced
30 ml | 1 fl. oz vegetable oil
80 g | 2 ½ oz mixed salad leaves
2 red apples, peeled and chopped
30 g | 1 oz chopped hazelnuts (cobnuts)
30 g | 1 oz pine nuts

Method:
Mix the vinegars, orange juice and olive oil together to make a dressing. Season with salt and pepper and set the dressing aside.

Cut each bacon rasher in half and wrap each slice of goat's cheese with 2 pieces of bacon, like a small parcel. Secure them with a cocktail stick.

Heat the vegetable oil in a large frying pan and gently fry the cheese until lightly browned, turning frequently.

Mix the salad leaves with the apples and toss with the dressing.

Arrange the dressed salad onto plates, add the goat's cheese, scatter over the hazelnuts and pine nuts.

Linguine alla genovese

serves: 4

Ingredients:
400 g | 14 oz ribbon pasta
100 g | 3 ½ oz | 1 cup pine nuts
200 g | 7 oz green (string) beans
1 bunch basil
3 cloves of garlic
50 g | 2 oz | ½ cup Parmesan, grated
100 ml | 3 ½ fl. oz olive oil
4 new potatoes, boiled and sliced

Method:
Heat a large pan of salted water to boiling point and cook the pasta according to packet instructions.

Toast the pine nuts in a dry pan until lightly browned. Set a few aside to garnish and place the remainder in a food processor.

Steam the beans until just tender then set aside. Reserve a few basil leaves to garnish and add the rest to the pine nuts. Add the Parmesan, garlic and oil and blend until you have a coarse paste. Season with salt and pepper.

When the pasta is cooked, drain well and stir in the sauce. Garnish with pine nuts, green beans and sliced potatoes to serve.

Thai red curry

serves: 4

Ingredients:
vegetable oil
600 g | 1 ¼ lbs beef steak,
cut into chunks
2 shallots, finely chopped
2 cloves of garlic, finely chopped
fresh ginger, peeled and grated
red curry paste
1 stalk lemongrass, sliced in
half lengthways
2 red chillies, sliced lengthways
1 tsp sugar
1 tbsp fish sauce
300 ml | 11 fl. oz | 1 ⅓ cups
coconut milk
400 ml | 14 fl. oz | 1 ⅔ cups beef stock
200 g | 7 oz green baby
aubergines (eggplants)
200 g | 7 oz cherry tomatoes
1 tbsp chopped coriander
Thai basil, chopped

Method:
Heat the oil in a large pan and add the shallots, garlic and ginger, cook for 2 minutes then add the curry paste, lemongrass and chillies. Add the meat and brown the meat on all sides.

Add the sugar, fish sauce, coconut milk, stock and aubergines and increase the heat to boiling point. Turn the heat down and simmer gently for 20 minutes.

Drop the cherry tomatoes into boiling water for 30 seconds, then peel off the skins and add the tomatoes to the curry with the coriander. Season with salt and pepper the chopped Thai basil, and serve with Thai jasmine rice.

Lamb chops with harissa and couscous

serves: 4

Ingredients:
180 g | 6 oz | 1 cup couscous
8 lamb chops, trimmed
60 g | 2 oz harissa
45 g | 1 ½ fl. oz olive oil
4 artichoke hearts, halved vertically
I lemon, juice and zest
2 red onions, thinly sliced into rings
250 g | 9 oz cherry tomatoes, halved
2 tbsp chopped parsley

Method:

Place the cous cous in a bowl and just cover it with boiling water. Cover the bowl with a tea towel and leave to stand for 10 minutes. Season with salt and pepper and fluff it up with a fork. Rub the lamb chops with the harissa and set aside.

Grease a griddle pan with a little of the oil and cook the artichoke hearts until lightly browned. Set them aside and keep warm.

Brush the pan with a little more oil and cook the lamb chops for about 6 minutes on each side, basting from time to time.

Meanwhile, cut the lemon zest into fine strips. Add the zest and juice along with the remaining oil, the onions, tomatoes and parsley and season with salt and pepper to the cous cous.

Serve the lamb chops on a bed of couscous with the artichoke.

Chicken with spinach and peppers

serves: 4

Ingredients:
200 g | 7 oz | 1 cup quinoa
75 ml | 2 ½ fl. oz olive oil
2 cloves of garlic, crushed
1 red chilli, finely chopped
4 red peppers, chopped
2 tomatoes, chopped
2 handfuls spinach, washed
4 small chicken breasts, skinned

Method:
Cook the quinoa in a pan of boiling, salted water for 15 minutes, until the grains look like little spirals, drain and set aside.

To make the sauce heat 3 tablespoons of oil in a pan and gently cook the garlic and chilli for 2 minutes, stirring all the time.

Add the peppers, cook for 5 minutes then add the tomatoes, reduce the heat and simmer for 20 minutes. Season with salt and pepper.

Put the spinach in a large pan with a lid and cook until it begins to wilt. Drain well, squeeze out excess moisture and keep warm.

Flatten the chicken breasts with a meat hammer or rolling pin. Heat the remaining oil in a wide frying pan, cook the chicken breasts until lightly brown. Remove from the pan, put a little spinach on the cooked side of each one and secure with a cocktail stick.

Return to the pan carefully and cook gently for about 5 minutes or until the chicken is cooked through.

Serve the chicken on top of the quinoa with the pepper sauce.

Sausage and vegetable casserole

serves: 4

Ingredients:
90 ml | 3 fl. oz oil
8 sausages
1 onion, finely chopped
1 clove of garlic, chopped
1 red pepper, chopped
1 green pepper, chopped
1 yellow pepper, chopped
90 oz | 3 oz new potatoes, scrubbed and halved
400 g | 14 oz | 2 cups tomatoes, canned
125 ml | 4 ½ fl. oz | ½ cup vegetable stock
200 g | 7 oz cherry tomatoes

Method:

Heat 2 tablespoons of the oil in a large frying pan and fry the sausages over a medium heat until browned on all sides.

Heat the remaining oil in a large saucepan. Add the onions and cook gently until they start to soften then add the garlic, peppers and potatoes.

Cook for 3 minutes, stirring all the time, then add the canned tomatoes and stock. Increase the heat to boiling point, then turn the heat down and gently simmer for 10 minutes.

Add the cherry tomatoes and sausages, season with salt and pepper and continue cooking until the vegetables are soft and the sausage are cooked through.

Spicy king prawns

serves: 4

Ingredients:
600 g | 1 ½ lb raw king prawns, peeled
1 tbsp groundnut oil
small piece fresh ginger, grated
1 tsp Sichuan pepper
2 cloves of garlic, crushed
2 spring onions, trimmed and chopped
1 tbsp tomato puree
2 tsp chilli bean sauce
1 tsp cider vinegar
1 tsp sugar
2 tsp sesame oil
coriander (cilantro) leaves, to garnish

Method:
Cut the fine black vein from the prawns, wash and dry them on kitchen paper. Heat the oil in a wok, add the ginger, Sichuan pepper and garlic and stir fry for 30 seconds.

Add the prawns and stir fry for 1 minute. Add the tomato puree, chilli bean sauce, cider vinegar, sugar and sesame oil and stir fry for another few minutes.

Serve with jasmine rice, garnished with coriander.

Spinach and potato tortilla

serves: 1

Ingredients:
30 ml | 1 fl. oz olive oil
100 g | 3 ½ oz new potatoes,
boiled and sliced
2 eggs
1 handful baby spinach, washed

Method:
Heat the oil in a 15 cm / 6 " frying pan and saute the potatoes for 15 minutes until lightly browned.

Whisk the eggs in a cup and season with salt and pepper. Pour over the potatoes and scatter with the spinach.

Cover the pan and cook over a low to medium heat for about 4 minutes, or until the egg has set.

Spicy sour prawn soup

serves: 4

Ingredients:
45 ml | 1 ½ fl. oz sesame oil
2 shallots, finely chopped
2 spring onions (scallions),
finely chopped
2 red chillies, finely chopped
2 cloves of garlic, chopped
750 ml | 26 fl. oz | 3 cups fish stock
30 ml | 1 fl. oz dark soy sauce
1 lime, juiced
1 tbsp fish sauce
1 tsp sugar
450 g | 16 oz king prawns
200 g | 7 oz rice noodles
coriander (cilantro), chopped

Method:
Heat the oil in a large pan and gently cook the shallots and spring onions over a low heat until soft.

Add the chilli and garlic, cook for 2 minutes then add the stock and bring to a simmer. Add the soy sauce, lime juice, fish sauce and sugar and allow it to simmer for a few minutes. Add the prawns and rice noodles and simmer gently for 5 minutes.

Serve garnished with the chopped coriander.

Pollo alla cacciatora

serves: 4

Ingredients:
45 ml | 1 ½ fl. oz oil
1 onion, finely chopped
2 cloves of garlic
4 thick rashers bacon, chopped
200 g | 7 oz | 2 cups mushrooms, sliced
125 ml | 4 ½ fl. oz | ½ cup white wine
400 g | 14 oz | 4 cups tomatoes, canned
8 pieces chicken, cooked
1 tsp parsley, chopped
1 tsp rosemary, chopped

Method:
Heat the oil in a large pan. Add the onions and garlic, cook gently for 5 minutes then add the bacon and cook it until the fat starts to run, then add the mushrooms.

Cook for 3 minutes and add the wine, let it bubble then add the tomatoes and increase the heat to boiling point.

Add the chicken, season with salt and pepper and turn the heat down to a simmer. Cook for 10-15 minutes sprinkle the parsley and rosemary.

Chicken breast with mushrooms

serves: 4

Ingredients:
4 large floury potatoes,
peeled and chopped
45 ml | 1 ½ fl. oz sesame oil
30 ml | 1 fl. oz honey
1 tsp ground ginger
2 large chicken breasts, skinned
½ Savoy cabbage, shredded
100 g | 3 ½ oz | 1 stick butter
200 g | 7 oz oyster
mushrooms, chopped
45 ml | 1 ½ fl. oz vegetable oil
125 ml | 4 ½ fl. oz | ½ cup milk

Method:
Boil the potatoes in a large pan of salted water for 15 minutes until soft. Mix the sesame oil, honey and ginger together and rub into the chicken breasts.

Quickly steam or boil the cabbage until just tender, then set it aside. Heat a large frying pan and gently fry the mushrooms until they are tender and lightly browned. Remove them from the pan and set aside.

Wipe the pan clean with kitchen paper and add the vegetable oil, and increase to a high heat. Add the chicken breasts and cook for 4-5 minutes on each side, or until cooked through.

When the potatoes are cooked, drain them well, then return them to the pan and mash until smooth with the remaining butter and the milk, and season with salt and pepper.

Cut each chicken breast in half and serve with the mashed potato, cabbage and mushrooms.

Thai green chicken curry

serves: 4

Ingredients:
8 chicken thighs, skinned,
boned and sliced
30 ml | 1 fl. oz oil
30 g | 1 oz green curry paste
1 stalk lemongrass, finely chopped
2 shallots, finely chopped
2 cloves of garlic, finely chopped
4 kaffir lime leaves
2 tbsp fresh ginger, peeled and grated
1 tsp sugar
1 tbsp fish sauce
300 ml | 11 fl. oz | 1 ⅓ cups
coconut milk
400 ml | 14 fl. oz | 1 ⅔ cups
chicken stock
100 g | 3 ½ oz baby aubergines
(eggplants)
100 g | 3 ½ oz green (string) beans
Thai basil, to garnish
Coriander (cilantro) leaves, to garnish

Method:
Heat the oil in a large pan and cook the chicken for
1-2 minutes, until golden brown.

Add the curry paste, lemongrass, shallots, garlic, kaffir lime
leaves, ginger and sugar.

Cook for 2 minutes then stir in the fish sauce, coconut milk and
chicken stock.

Add the aubergines and simmer gently for 15 minutes. Add the
green beans, and cook for 3 minutes. Add fish sauce, salt to
taste and the coriander leaves. Serve with Thai jasmine rice.

dinner.

Egg, bacon and potato rosti

serves: 4

Ingredients:
6 large floury potatoes,
peeled and halved
75 ml | 2 ½ fl. oz oil
8 rashers bacon, chopped
2 sprigs rosemary, finely chopped
4 eggs

Method:
Place the potatoes in a large pan of salted water and boil
for 5 minutes.

Heat 2 tablespoons of oil in a large frying pan and fry the
bacon until browned and crisp. Remove the bacon from
the pan and keep warm.

Drain the potatoes, let them stand for a minute, then mix in
most of the rosemary, leaving a little for the garnish, season
with salt and pepper and break the potatoes up with a fork.
Shape the potato into small patties with your hands.

Add the remaining oil to the pan. Fry the rosti gently for about
3 minutes each side or until golden brown and cooked through.
Remove from the pan, drain on kitchen paper and keep warm.

Carefully break the eggs into the pan and gently fry for
3-4 minutes, then return the rosti to the pan, top with the eggs
and add the bacon and reserved rosemary to the pan.

Grilled tuna and lentil salad

serves: 4

Ingredients:
4 tuna steaks
45 ml | 1 ½ fl. oz olive oil
2 tsp black peppercorns, lightly crushed
1 clove of garlic, chopped
1 tbsp juniper berries, lightly crushed
2 limes, juiced

For the lentil salad:
400 g | 14 oz | 2 cups
green lentils, canned
1 red onion, finely chopped
2 red chillies, finely chopped
1 clove of garlic, finely chopped
45 ml | 1 ½ fl. oz olive oil
1 tbsp white wine vinegar
mayonnaise, to serve
fresh coriander (cilantro)
lime wedges

Method:
For the lentil salad, mix the lentils, onion, chilli peppers, garlic, oil and vinegar together. Season with salt and pepper and set aside.

Wash and dry the tuna steaks and place them in a flat dish. Mix the remaining ingredients together pour over the tuna. Mix well and set them aside to marinade for 15 minutes.

Heat an oiled griddle pan on a high heat and cook the tuna for about 3 minutes on each side. Spoon over the marinade and baste for the last 2 minutes of cooking.

Serve the tuna with the lentil salad with the mayonnaise, coriander and lime wedges.

Creamy seafood stew

serves: 4

Ingredients:
30 g | 1 oz butter
30 ml | 1 fl. oz vegetable oil
2 leeks, thinly sliced
250 g | 9 oz bacon, thickly sliced
and chopped
750 ml | 26 fl. oz | 3 cups fish stock
4 potatoes, peeled and cut into chunks
450 g | 1 lb sea bass fillets,
cut into chunks
450 g | 1 lb mussels, cleaned and
beards removed
250 ml | 9 fl. oz | 1 cup cream
2 tbsp parsley, chopped

Method:
Melt the butter and oil in large saucepan and gently cook the leeks for 3 minutes.

Add the bacon, cook for 2 minutes then add the stock and potatoes and increase the heat to boiling point.

Simmer for 15 minutes then add the sea bass and mussels, cover the pan with a lid and cook for 3 minutes or until the mussels have opened.

Remove the mussels from their shells and return them to the pan, discarding any mussels that have not opened.

Add the cream, season with salt and pepper and return to a simmer. Season the pan with salt and pepper and add the chopped parsley.

Moroccan meatballs with couscous

serves: 4

Ingredients:
60 ml | 2 fl. oz oil
1 onion, very finely chopped
1 clove of garlic, finely chopped
1 tsp ground cumin
600 g | 1 ¼ lbs minced (ground) lamb
1 egg
30 g | 1 oz harissa

For the couscous:
180 g | 6 oz | 1 cup couscous
2 carrots, finely chopped
150 g | 5 oz | 1 cup chickpeas
(garbanzos), canned
6 spring onions (scallions), sliced
1 red chilli, chopped
2 tbsp chopped parsley
45 ml | 1 ½ fl. oz olive oil
½ lemon, juiced
30 g | 1 oz rocket (arugula)

Method:
Cover the couscous with just enough boiling water and set it aside for 10 minutes.

For the meatballs, heat a little of the oil in a large frying pan and cook the onion and garlic for 2 minutes over a medium heat. Add the cumin and cook for another minute.

Place the lamb in a large bowl, add the onion mixture, the egg and harissa, and season with salt and pepper. Shape the mixture into meatballs with your hands.

Wipe the pan clean with kitchen paper, add the remaining oil and gently fry the meatballs for about 10 minutes or until cooked through. Stir them frequently to ensure even cooking.

Fluff the couscous with a fork and mix in the remaining ingredients. Season with salt and pepper and serve topped with the meatballs.

Beef curry

serves: 4

Ingredients:
45 ml | 1 ½ fl. oz vegetable oil
2 cloves of garlic, finely sliced
small piece fresh ginger,
peeled and finely sliced
45 g | 1 ½ oz yellow curry paste
600 g | 1 ½ lb beef steak, thinly sliced
500 ml | 18 fl. oz | 2 cups beef
stock or water
400 ml | 14 fl. oz | 1 ½ cups
coconut milk
12 Thai basil leaves
1 lime, juiced

Method:
Heat the oil in a large pan and gently fry the garlic until soft.
Add the ginger, stir in the curry paste and cook for 2 minutes.

Add the beef, stir for 2 minutes then add the stock, coconut
milk and Thai basil leaves. Increase the heat to boiling point,
then simmer for 15 minutes until the beef is cooked through.

Stir in the lime juice, season with salt and pepper and serve
with basmati rice.

Penne alla caprese

serves: 4

Ingredients:
400 g | 14 oz penne
125 ml | 4 ½ fl. oz | ½ cup olive oil
2 red onions, finely sliced
2 cloves of garlic, chopped
1 red chilli, chopped
800 g | 1 ¾ lb | 4 cups canned tomatoes
1 tbsp chopped parsley
250 g | 9 oz | 2 cups mozzarella, cubed
4 sprigs basil, shredded

Method:
Heat a large pan of salted water to boiling point and cook the penne for 10-15 minutes. Heat the oil in a large frying pan and cook the onions over a fairly high heat until they have softened and started to caramelise.

Add the garlic and chilli, cook for 2 minutes then add the tomatoes, heat to boiling point and simmer for 15 minutes until the sauce has reduced and thickened. Season with salt and freshly ground black pepper.

When the penne is cooked, drain well and add to the frying pan with the parsley and mozzarella and season the pan generously with salt and pepper. Mix well and garnish with basil before serving.

dessert.

Raspberry trifle

serves: 4

Ingredients:
350 ml | 12 fl. oz | 1 ½ cups cream
500 g | 18 oz chocolate ice-cream
150 g | 5 oz ginger biscuits
(cookies), crumbled
250 g | 9 oz | 2 cups fresh raspberries

Method:
Whip the cream until it forms stiff peaks.

Put half of the ice-cream into a large glass bowl and smooth it gently. Scatter with half of the biscuits and press down slightly.

Add half of the cream and half of the raspberries. Next, add the rest of the ice-cream and the rest of the biscuits and finish with a layer of cream. Scatter the remaining raspberries on top, place the trifle into the freezer for 10 minutes and then serve immediately.

Spicy fruit salad

serves: 4

Ingredients:
2 star anise
1 lime, zest
1 cinnamon stick
4 cloves
110 g | 4 oz | ½ cup sugar
1 can pineapple chunks
1 papaya, peeled,
deseeded and diced
2 star fruits, sliced
2 mandarin oranges,
peeled and segmented
1 pink grapefruit,
peeled and segmented
1 mango, peeled,
stone removed and diced
2 kiwi fruits, peeled and chopped
60 g | 2 oz pomegranate seeds
50 g | 2 oz | ½ cup redcurrants
50 g | 2 oz | ½ cup small black grapes

Method:

Drain the pineapple chunks for the salad and pour their syrup into a measuring jug. Add enough water to make the liquid up to 500 ml.

Place the liquid in a small saucepan with the star anise, zest of lime, cinnamon stick, cloves and sugar. Heat to boiling point, then simmer for 10 minutes and strain using a fine sieve.

Place all the fruity in a large bowl, pour over the warm syrup and mix. Serve warm or cold.

Banana and sesame fritters

serves: 4

Ingredients:

30 g | 1 oz sesame seeds
vegetable oil, for deep-frying
200 g | 7 oz | 2 cups self-raising flour
2 tsp bicarbonate of soda
(baking soda)
2 eggs
ice-cold sparkling water
6 bananas
vanilla ice-cream

Method:

Toast the sesame seeds in a dry pan until lightly browned then coarsely grind them with a pestle and mortar or small food processor.

Put the oil in a deep pan to a depth of about 8 cm / 3 " and bring it to a high heat.

Beat the ground sesame seeds, flour, bicarbonate of soda and eggs together with enough sparkling water to form a loose batter.

The oil is hot enough when bubbles appear on a wooden spoon dipped into the pan. Slice the bananas in half diagonally, dip in the batter and deep-fry in batches until golden brown.

Drain the banana fritters on kitchen paper and serve with the ice-cream.

Raspberry cranachan

serves: 4

Ingredients:
400 g | 14 oz | 3 cups fresh raspberries
60 g | 2 oz icing (confectioners') sugar
500 ml | 18 fl. oz | 2 cups cream
90 g | 3 oz | 1 cup coarse oatmeal
icing (confectioners') sugar, to garnish

Method:
Puree half of the raspberries with half of the sugar and a little water and pass through a fine sieve.

Lightly whip the cream and fold in the remaining sugar and the oatmeal.

Layer the remaining raspberries into serving glasses with the raspberry puree and the cream and oatmeal mixture.

Dust with icing sugar and serve immediately.

Tarte citron minute

serves: 4

Ingredients:
450 g | 1 lb ready-made sweet pastry
200 g | 7 oz | 1 cup lemon curd
30 g | 1 oz icing (confectioners') sugar

Method:

Heat the oven to 200°C (180° fan) 400F, gas 6.

Roll out the pastry to a 5 mm / ¼ " thickness and cut 8 circles, 8 cm / 3" diameter. Line greased mini tart pans with the pastry circles.

Spoon the lemon curd into the pastry cases and bake in the oven for 10-15 minutes until the pastry is golden brown.

Dust the edges of the tarts with icing sugar and serve warm or cold.

dessert.

Fruit skewers with chocolate sauce

serves: 4

Ingredients:
200 g | 7 oz dark chocolate,
broken into pieces
75 g | 2 ½ oz | ⅓ cup sugar
125 ml | 4 ½ fl. oz | ½ cup cream
60 ml | 2 fl. oz water
2 bananas
1 lemon, juiced
2 kiwi fruit, peeled and thickly sliced
12 large strawberries, halved
½ a small pineapple, peeled,
cored and cut into chunks

Method:
Place the chocolate, sugar, cream and water in a small pan and gently heat until smooth and thick.

Peel the banana, cut into slices and mix with the lemon juice to prevent the banana browning.

Thread the banana, kiwi, strawberries and pineapple chunks onto wooden skewers and serve with the chocolate sauce.

Raspberry tiramisu

serves: 4

Ingredients:
12 sponger fingers (ladyfingers)
45 ml | 1 ½ fl. oz sweet white wine
30 ml | 1 fl. oz espresso
450 g | 1 lb | 2 cups mascarpone
1 tbsp icing (confectioners') sugar
1 tbsp lemon juice
400 g | 14 oz | 3 cups fresh raspberries
75 g | 2 ½ oz dark chocolate

Method:
Break the sponge fingers into pieces and divide them between 4 serving dishes.

Drizzle the espresso over the sponge with a little of the sweet wine, then add the remaining wine to the mascarpone with the sugar and lemon juice and beat together until smooth.

Spoon a little of the mascarpone cream over the sponge fingers, finely grate some of the chocolate on top, then arrange a ring of raspberries around the dish.

Spoon on the remaining mascarpone cream, top with the remaining raspberries and grate the rest of the chocolate to finish.

Rice pudding

serves: 4

Ingredients:
100 g | 3 ½ oz | ½ cup pudding rice
60 g | 2 oz sugar
750 ml | 26 fl. oz | 3 cups milk
30 ml | 1 fl. oz cream
1 tsp ground cinnamon

Method:
Rinse the rice in a sieve under running water and place in a saucepan.

Add the sugar and milk and increase the heat to boiling point. Cook for 20-25 minutes, stirring frequently, or until the rice is tender. You may need to add a little more milk.

Spoon the pudding into the bowls, with the cream on top. Sprinkle the rice pudding with cinnamon and serve.

Pear tarte tatin

serves: 4

Ingredients:
800 g | 1 ¾ lbs pear halves, canned
30 ml | 1 fl. oz lemon juice
30 g | 1 oz brown sugar
45 g | 1 ½ oz butter
450 g | 1 lb ready-rolled puff pastry,
thawed if frozen

Method:

Heat the oven to 220°C (200° fan) 425F, gas 7.

Drain the pear halves, pouring the liquid into a small pan. Cut the pear halves in half again and set them aside.

Add the lemon juice and sugar to the pan and increase the heat to boiling point.

Melt the butter in a large, ovenproof frying pan, allow it to bubble, then arrange the pear quarters around the pan.

Pour the syrup over and let it simmer while you cut a circle of pastry slightly larger than the pan. Place the pastry on top of the pan, tucking in the edges, then transfer the pan to the oven and bake for 15 minutes or until the pastry is golden brown.

Carefully upturn the tart onto a serving plate and serve with ice-cream or crème fraiche.

Strawberry meringue

serves: 4

Ingredients:
225 g | 8 oz | 1 cup cream cheese
3 tbsp low-fat yoghurt
½ tsp vanilla extract
16 strawberries, hulled and halved
8 meringues
30 g | 1 oz icing (confectioners') sugar

Method:
Beat the cream cheese, yoghurt and vanilla extract together until smooth.

Arrange the strawberries and meringues onto serving plates, pour over the cheese mixture and dust with the icing sugar.

Baked peaches with almonds

serves: 4

Ingredients:
4 ripe peaches
75 g | 2 ½ oz | ½ cup ground almonds
4 amaretti biscuits, crumbled
60 g | 2 oz dark muscovado sugar
100 ml | 3 ½ fl. oz cream

Method:
Preheat the oven to 200°C (180° fan) 400F, gas 6.

Cut the peaches in half and remove the stones. Mix the almonds, crumbled amaretti biscuits and sugar and fill the cavities of the peaches with the mixture.

Place the filled peaches in a small roasting pan and bake in the oven for 10-15 minutes.

While the peaches are cooking, lightly whip the cream and serve alongside the baked peaches.

dessert.

Strawberries with white chocolate sauce

serves: 4

Ingredients:
500 ml | 18 fl. oz | 2 cups cream
100 g | 3 ½ oz white chocolate,
broken into pieces
450 g | 1 lb strawberries, halved
100 g | 3 ½ oz | 1 ¼ cups flaked
(slivered) almonds

Method:
Place half of the cream in a small saucepan and very gently simmer.

Add the chocolate and the remaining cream to the pan, stirring all the time, until the chocolate has melted and the sauce is thick and creamy.

Place the strawberries into serving bowls, pour over the sauce and scatter over the almonds.

Lime chiffon pie

serves: 4

Ingredients:
300 g | 11 oz | 3 cups crushed
digestive biscuits (graham crackers)
100 g | 3 ½ oz | 1 stick butter, melted
1 packet lime-flavoured
jelly (jello), dissolved in hot water
2 egg whites, whipped until stiff
30 g | 1 oz caster (superfine) sugar
300 ml | 10 fl. oz | 1 ¼ cup cream
whipped until stiff
2 limes, zest only
lime slices

Method:
Mix the melted butter into the biscuit crumbs and press the mixture into a greased 20 cm / 8 " pie dish and chill while the filling is made.

Fold the chilled jelly mixture into the whipped egg whites and carefully fold in the sugar, most of the whipped cream and lime zest. Pour the mixture into the pie dish and chill in the freezer for 20 minutes.

Carefully remove the pie from the dish and serve garnished with the remaining whipped cream and lime slices.

Summer fruit pancakes

serves: 4

Ingredients:
150 g | 5 oz | 1 ½ cups plain (all-purpose) flour
100 ml | 3 ½ fl. oz milk
2 eggs
45 ml | 1 ½ fl. oz vegetable oil

For the raspberry sauce:
200 g | 7 oz | 1 ½ cups raspberries
1 tsp lemon juice
30 g | 1 oz icing (confectioners') sugar

To serve:
400 g | 14 oz | 3 cups blackberries, raspberries and blueberries

Method:
Whisk the flour, milk and eggs together with 150 ml of water until it forms a smooth batter and set it aside.

For the coulis, puree the raspberries with a splash of water. Add the lemon juice and icing sugar then pass it through a fine sieve and set it aside.

Heat a little of the oil in a frying pan over a medium heat and add a ladleful of the pancake mixture, tilting the pan to cover the base. Cook the pancake for 2 minutes, then flip over and cook for 2 more minutes.

Repeat with the remaining pancake mixture, placing the pancakes between sheets of baking parchment and keep warm. Fill the pancakes with berries, fold and serve drizzled with raspberry sauce.

Blackcurrant trifle

serves: 4

Ingredients:
8 sponge fingers (ladyfingers)
30 ml | 1 fl. oz white rum
30 ml | 1 fl. oz lemon juice
250 ml | 9 fl. oz | 1 cup cream
150 g | 5 oz | ¾ cup low-fat
cream cheese
45 g | 1 ½ oz sugar
200 g | 7 oz | 2 cups frozen
blackcurrants, thawed
1-2 tbsp icing (confectioners') sugar
50 g | 2 oz flaked (slivered) almonds

Method:
Crumble the sponge fingers and divide them between 4 glasses. Mix the rum with the lemon juice and sprinkle over the sponge fingers.

Whip the cream until it forms stiff peaks. Beat the cream cheese with the sugar and fold in the cream. Spoon the cream on top of the sponge fingers.

Mix the blackcurrants with the icing sugar, spoon over the cream and sprinkle with flaked almonds.

Strawberry meringue

serves: 4

Ingredients:
300 g | 11 oz | 1 ½ cups
strawberries, diced
1 lime, juiced and zest
30 ml | 1 fl. oz rum
4 scoops vanilla ice-cream
2 egg whites
45 g | 1 ½ oz icing
(confectioners') sugar

Method:
Preheat the grill to a high setting.

Mix the strawberries with the lime juice, zest and rum and pour into 4 ramekins. Place a scoop of vanilla ice-cream on top of each.

Beat the egg whites until they form stiff peaks and gradually fold in the icing sugar.

Place the meringue gently on top of the ice-cream so that everything is covered and then grill for 6-8 minutes until golden brown.

Fruit salad

serves: 4

Ingredients:
1 cantaloupe melon
200 g | 7 oz | 2 cups red grapes, halved
50 g | 2 oz strawberries
50 g | 2 oz pineapple
30 ml | 1 fl. oz lemon juice
200 g | 7 oz low-fat Greek yoghurt
30 ml | 1 fl. oz honey
2 tbsp linseeds

Method:
Chop the peeled and deseeded melon, halve the grapes and slice the strawberries and pineapple into bite-size pieces. Divide the fruit salad into serving bowls.

Mix the honey, Greek yoghurt and lemon juice together and spoon over the fruit. Sprinkle with the linseeds.

dessert.

Eton mess

serves: 4

Ingredients:
450 g | 1 lb strawberries, quartered
30 g | 1 oz icing (confectioners') sugar
250 ml | 9 fl. oz | 1 cup cream
4 meringue nests, crumbled

Method:
Puree half of the strawberries with the sugar and a little water in a food processor and pass them through a fine sieve.

Lightly whip the cream until it holds soft peaks.

Layer the crumbled meringue into serving glasses with the whipped cream and remaining strawberries. Drizzle over the strawberry puree and serve immediately.

Strawberry and yoghurt pastries

serves: 2

Ingredients:
4 sheets filo pastry
25 g | 1 oz | ¼ stick butter, melted
30 g | 1 oz sugar
250 ml | 9 fl. oz | 1 cup yoghurt
1 tbsp runny honey
250 g | 9 oz strawberries, sliced
1 orange, zest only

Method:
Heat the oven to 220°C (200° fan) 425F, gas 7.

Using scissors, cut each sheet of filo pastry into 8 pieces.
Brush 2 baking trays with a little melted butter, place the pastry pieces on the sheet and brush them with more butter.

Sprinkle with a little sugar and bake in the oven for 5 minutes or until lightly browned and crisp.

Mix the yogurt with the honey and gently mix in most of the strawberry slices, setting a few aside.

Place 8 pieces of cooked pastry onto each plate. Carefully spoon over the yoghurt and strawberry mixture, add a few reserved strawberry slices then top with 8 more pastry pieces and scatter over the orange zest.

Warm pear tartlets

serves: 4

Ingredients:
450 g | 1 lb ready-rolled puff pastry
2 cans pear halves, drained
30 g | 1 oz butter, melted
30 g | 1 oz icing (confectioners') sugar
250 ml | 9 fl. oz | 1 cup cream

Method:
Heat the oven to 220°C (200° fan) 425F, gas 7.

Cut circles from the pastry slightly bigger than the length of the pear halves. Place the pastry circles on a greased baking tray and brush the tops with melted butter.

Place a pear half in the centre of each pastry circle, press them down gently and bake in the oven for 5 minutes until puffed up and golden brown.

Meanwhile, gently whip the cream until it forms soft peaks. Dust the tartlets which icing sugar and serve with whipped cream.

index

index.

index.